Ten Tiny Fingers, Nine Tiny To

Sue Townsend's new tragicomedy
only the upper strata of society are
children must be perfect specimens if they are to live.

Ten Tiny Fingers, Nine Tiny Toes was first staged at the Library
Theatre, Manchester in November 1989.

Sue Townsend lives in Leicester. Her plays include **Womberang**
(Soho Poly, London, 1979); **Dayroom** (Croydon Warehouse
Theatre, 1981); **The Ghost of Daniel Lambert** (Leicester Phoenix,
1981); **Bazaar and Rummage** (Royal Court Theatre Upstairs,
1982, BBC Television, 1983); **Groping for Words** (Croydon
Warehouse, 1983); **The Great Celestial Cow** (The Joint Stock
Company, 1984); **The Secret Diary of Adrian Mole aged 13 ¾ –
The Play** (Leicester Phoenix, 1984), and **Ten Tiny Fingers, Nine
Tiny Toes** (Library Theatre, Manchester, 1989). Her other
published work includes **The Secret Diary of Adrian Mole Aged
13 ¾** (1982); **The Secret Diary of Adrian Mole Songbook** (in
collaboration with Ken Howard and Alan Blaikley, 1985); **The
Growing Pains of Adrian Mole** (1984) and **The True
Confessions of Adrian Albert Mole** (1989). Her novel
Rebuilding Coventry was published in 1988.

Sue Townsend

Ten Tiny Fingers, Nine Tiny Toes

Methuen Drama

A Methuen Modern Play

First published in Great Britain in 1990 by Methuen Drama,
Methuen Publishing Ltd, 215 Vauxhall Bridge Road,
London SW1V 1EJ

10 9 8 7 6 5 4

Copyright © 1990 Sue Townsend

A CIP catalogue record for this book is available from
the British Library

Methuen Publishing Ltd Reg No. 3543167

ISBN 0–413–61760–2

The photograph on the front cover is of the Library Theatre,
Manchester production with Lou Wakefield as Lucinda and Ruth
Sheen as Dot. (© John Haynes) The photograph of Sue Townsend
on the back cover is by Tessa Musgrave.

Printed and bound in Great Britain
by Cox & Wyman Ltd, Reading, Berkshire

Introduction

Ten Tiny Fingers was written four years ago. The title came from
the song that the Beverley Sisters used to sing: 'Twenty Tiny
Fingers – Twenty Tiny Toes'. The song is very catchy and oozes
sentiment. The sisters sing of a world where babies have 'cute kiss
curls', 'angels faces' and 'turned up noses'.

I've had four babies and they all sprang from the womb scowling
and bald and angry looking. It took time to love them, though
nobody could say I didn't care for them; I checked their pulses and
stood over them as they slept; I agonized over the temperature of
their room, and the quantity and quality of their food. In other
words I turned into a normal neurotic mother. I would hand wrestle
a tiger to save each of my children from its jaws.

This play is about the fierce and overpowering love that *most* women
feel for their children both born and unborn. It is set in the future in
a world where babies are bought and sold and even advertised by a
totalitarian government. The play is a modern melodrama and
teeters on a dangerous tightrope of laughter and tears. One big man
left the production at Manchester dabbing his eyes and saying to his
female companions, 'You'll have to excuse me, I don't usually show
my emotions'.
  I would like to dedicate this play to all imperfect babies and all
imperfect adults. As Lucinda says in the play, 'What's a missing
toe?'.

Sue Townsend
Leicester
September 1990

Ten Tiny Fingers, Nine Tiny Toes was first performed at the Library Theatre, Manchester on 3 November 1989 with the following cast:

Lucinda Darling	Lou Wakefield
Ralph Darling	Brian Capron
Dorothy Bird	Ruth Sheen
Peter Bird	Ian Mercer
Orderly	Tracie Bennett
Alan Cathcart/Mr Crudwell/Vassal	Simon Pearsall
Police Officer/Priest/Judge	Jo Cameron Brown

Directed by Carole Hayman
Designed by Claudia Mayer
Lighting designed by Jenny Cane

Scenes

Scene One	February – The Cairngorms
Scene Two	April – Derbyshire
Scene Three	The Salesman's Office
Scene Four	The Conception Ceremony
Scene Five	The Fertilisation Ceremony
Scene Six	The Tower Block
Scene Seven	High Ground – Derbyshire
Scene Eight	Buxton Maternity Unit
Scene Nine	The Tower Block
Scene Ten	The Golf Course
Scene Eleven	Buxton Maternity Unit
Scene Twelve	The Delivery Room
Scene Thirteen	Buxton Maternity Unit

The play is set in the year 2001.

Scene One

The Year 2001

The Cairngorms, February. Snow on the Ground.

Ralph *and* **Lucinda** *are changing into ski-ing gear in the back of a hatchback car.*

Lucinda (*pulling on salopettes*) You shouldn't have laughed at that person with the sticking out teeth, he saw you.

Ralph Ah c'mon, you laughed yourself.

Lucinda Not out loud I didn't. I had the good manners to snigger quietly to myself.

Ralph He's got no right to have teeth like that.

Lucinda He can't help his teeth Ralph, he didn't ask for them did he? He hasn't been to a dentist and said, 'Here's my wallet, I want a set of teeth that people will laugh at in hotel dining rooms at 8.15 in the morning'.

Ralph And he hasn't been to a dentist and said, 'Gimme new teeth', either has he? He's obviously got the money.

Lucinda Ralph. No amount of orthodontic expertise could help that man. That's why it's incumbent on spectators *not* to laugh. His poor wife!

Ralph Poor? She'd paid at least ten grand a piece for those tits. You could ski down them. It'd be a bloody sight warmer an' all.

Lucinda Ralph! Keep your voice down, we're in Aviemore.

Ralph We're not in *Aviemore* Lucinda, we're in the Cairngorms. When you are asked where we've been you say we've been ski-ing *in the Cairngorms.*

Lucinda Not yet we haven't.

Ralph When we get back, we have. If anyone asks.

Lucinda We have to pass *through* Aviemore to get here.

Ralph But we don't stop.

Lucinda Well I think Aviemore looks nice. Tasteful. Chalets and greenery and stuff. A pizza parlour . . .

Ralph We won't be stopping. Do you know what the incidence of VD is in Aviemore?

Lucinda Of course I don't, how would I?

Ralph It's high Lucinda. Mega high.

Lucinda How do you know?

Ralph I read it.

Lucinda Where? We read the same paper. I didn't read it.

Ralph I read it in a book.

Lucinda You haven't got a book.

Ralph I had a book – once.

Lucinda When? I've never known you have a book.

Ralph Before we met.

Lucinda We've been married forever . . .

Ralph So?

Lucinda So the statistics are out of date. You're wrong Ralph, admit it.

Ralph Aviemore has mega VD statistics. The *queue* goes out of the door, I *know*.

Lucinda *puts her ski jacket on. She zips it up.*

Lucinda Oh Jesus . . . God.

Ralph What?

Lucinda You *came* here ski-ing. With Tom from work . . . Oh Jesus God . . . You got VD!

Ralph No I didn't. Tom did, I didn't.

Lucinda *starts to put her ski boots on now.*

Lucinda You didn't make love to me for months after you came back. You said you'd got a trauma because you saw a dead body brought down on the chair lift.

Ralph I did, I did. I'll never forget that shrouded figure.

Lucinda No Ralph. Not a shrouded figure – a naked figure. Somebody's naked figure. A girl's . . . a woman's . . . in your hotel room.

Ralph Lucinda . . .

Lucinda If Tom slept with a woman, then so did you. Oh Ralph, you did! You did! When Tom got a videophone you did. When Tom got his first hairweave, you did. Oh Ralph, you slept with a woman in Aviemore didn't you?

Ralph I didn't.

Lucinda You did. You got VD.

Ralph Keep your voice down. We're on the top of a bloody mountain, voices carry.

Lucinda Ralph, we're grown up married people. Tell me the truth. Tell me you got VD. Tell me. I can take it. Who was she? Young? Old? Fat? Thin? Infected? Who was she?

Ralph I don't even remember her name.

A long pause.

Lucinda Do my boots up. No I'm not . . . I don't . . .

He does her boots up.

Ralph Her name . . . escapes me. She was jolly.

Lucinda Jolly? You don't like jolly people. They irritate you.

Ralph I can't remember her name. I knew it.

They stand in ski boots.

Lucinda Hair?

Ralph Black.

Lucinda Length?

Ralph Short.

Lucinda Body?

Ralph Muscular, knotted calf muscles. I remember that.

Lucinda Jesus.

Ralph Twice. I only screwed her twice. (*Pause. Defensively.*) I was here for five days! (*Pause.*) Marion . . . (*He clicks his fingers.*) . . . Marion, that was her name.

Lucinda Marion. Jolly Marion. You preferred her to *me*?

They clomp about in the boots.

Ralph No! You were in Manchester, and Marion was here, in the Cairngorms.

Lucinda Ralph, you were married to me.

Ralph C'mon Luce. I'm sorry, I am. She was lousy, it was a disaster both times.

Lucinda I believed you, about that body, about how it gave you that trauma and shrivelled your dick up.

Ralph She was horrible, *I* was drunk. *She* was drunk.

Lucinda Have you seen her since?

Ralph No. She went back to Japan.

Lucinda Japan! What was she doing, going to Japan?

Ralph She was Japanese! *Is* Japanese.

Lucinda With a name like Marion?

Ralph She was Japanese!

Lucinda Japanese people are not called Marion, and they do not have vp!

Ralph *You've* been with other men.

Lucinda No Ralph, I have not. Only you. Only you.

Pause.

Ralph Look, I've driven 300 bloody miles for this so let's go ski-ing shall we? Pick your skis up.

Lucinda No, I can't.

Ralph It's in the past.

Lucinda Not for me it's not. I've only just found out. The world has changed.

Ralph For Christ's sake!

Lucinda I wondered why we had to watch that telly series . . . the Japanese one . . . twelve boring weeks of it.

Ralph I haven't given her another thought.

Lucinda Japanese Marion. (*Pause.*) They were so cruel in that war.

Ralph She wasn't *born* in that war.

Lucinda Young was she?

Ralph Eighteen.

Lucinda (*despairingly*) Eighteen! Oh no Ralph, not 18. I can't compete with 18 . . .

Ralph Luce, how do I like my cheddar?

Lucinda What?

Ralph Cheddar cheese, I like it mature don't I? Same as women. So I had a brief flirtation.

Lucinda I'm going back.

Ralph To the hotel?

Lucinda No. To England.

Ralph Luce, you're over-reacting again.

Lucinda *picks up a ski stick and swipes* **Ralph** *with it.*

Lucinda I may kill you!

Ralph She doesn't count, she was a foreigner!

Lucinda Push you off the mountain!

Ralph When she came, she came in Japanese. It meant nothing to me . . . nothing. I couldn't understand what she was saying.

Lucinda You've never made *me* come.

Ralph Don't be silly, you have multi-orgasms three times a week.

Lucinda Prove it!

Ralph Well you have three *holidays* a year! Sex isn't everything!

Lucinda I want to come! I want to come! And, I want a baby.

Ralph People are looking. I'll *buy* you a baby. How much are they? Fetch my cheque book.

Lucinda Bloody Marion's got a baby I bet. There in soddin' Tokyo with slanty eyes and your chin. Yes, bleedin' Marion showing the kid your ski-ing photos. 'This is your father, son. One day we go back and meet him. His name Ralph, he big important boss of drinking straw factory in Derbyshire.'

Lucinda *knocks* **Ralph** *down, he lies on his back with his skis tangled together.*

Lucinda Cheerio Ralph. Sayonara.

Lucinda *clumps away offstage.*

Scene Two

Two months later

April in Derbyshire

Very high ground. In the far distance a group of six tower blocks. The sun is shining. There is a slight wind. A lamb bleats occasionally.

Dot *and* **Pete,** *a couple, dressed in ragged summer clothing, are dragging a pile of firewood on a plastic sack.*

Dot I shall have to stop.

They let go of the sack. **Dot** *drops onto the ground.* **Pete** *faces the audience looking at the view.*

Pete Ain't it nice Dot? Look how far away everything is.

Dot Lovely. (*She leans back and closes her eyes to let the sun to her face.*)

Pete My 'ands are black. Shall we stop at the river?

Dot River's in spate, you can't go swimming.

Pete Just a wash. (*Pause.*)

Pete There's lambs been born. I can see 'em.

Dot I can 'ear 'em. (*Pause.*) I can taste 'em.

They laugh gently.

Pete How many miles we done today?

Dot We been out 'bout four hours. 'Bout as long as that wood'll last on the fire.

Pete Don't need it today though.

Dot No. Oh it's lovely to be 'ot.

Pete 'An it's free.

Dot They can't sell the sunshine. Though I bet the buggers have put their minds to it.

Dot *undoes her blouse, she is wearing a dingy bra underneath. She lies full out, sunbathing. She pulls her skirt up to her thighs.*

Pete You look happy Dot.

Dot I am today.

Pete You like to be warm, don't you?

Dot Mmm.

Pete Don't go to sleep, I'll have to wake you if you do an' then you'll be mad at me.

Dot (*fondly*) You're as soft as shit. (*She sits up.*)

Pete You know that man that got hung?

Dot Yeah.

Pete Was it a sheep he stole or a lamb?

Dot It was a lamb. A dead 'un 'e found in a ditch, so don't get thinkin' . . .

Pete I weren't, I jus' wondered.

Dot Do you know who Eddie Cochran is Pete?

Pete No. Who is 'e?

Dot He was a singer. It's scratched on the lift door. 'Eddie Cochran lives.'

Pete Somebody took a chance.

Dot Daft. Fancy risking it.

She lies down again, sighing and stretching.

Pete *I'm* 'appy today. It was a good day's work that. Gettin' that wood. Can I lie next to you Dot?

Dot Mmm, oh that sun!

Pete *takes his coat and his trousers off. He lies on his back for a moment, and then turns towards* **Dot.**

Pete You look ever so nice. My hand keeps wanting to touch your skin.

Dot Let it.

Pete *strokes* **Dot***'s legs.*

Pete Wun't it be good, to build a house just 'ere?

Dot It'd be blown away once the wind got up.

Pete But wun't it be good? I'd put windows 'ere and 'ere . . . (*He indicates right and left and forward.*) . . . and a front door 'ere.

Dot What about there? (*She indicates towards the tower block.*)

Pete No, I wun't want to look at *them.* (*He turns to look at tower blocks.*)

I can see our room, the sun's shinin' on the winder. (*Pause*.) I'd 'ave a garden.

Dot We got one.

Pete No we ain't. Where?

Dot We're in it. It's ours, all this. Far as you can see.

She stands, looks.

Pete No, we're trespassin' 'ere. We're lawbreaking, I'm scared all the time we're out. Just in case. (*He kicks at the pile of wood*.) That's government wood.

Dot No it ain't. No more than the rocks is government, or the ridge, or the water in the river. They were here before they had a government and they'll be here when all the governments in the world have buggered off and left. It's all just . . . here. So don't be scared Pete, it was put here for all of us and we've just took our share that's all. I hate you when you say you're scared.

Pete I ain't really scared. Just worried. Don't 'ate me Dot.

Dot Well don't talk like that. Don't give in. Once you say you're scared or worried they've got you. They've took you over. They've got inside you and took over your brain and changed how you think. Be happy. Think about your garden. Your private garden. (*Laughing*.) You'd have a privet hedge wouldn't you? And conifers – you'd have conifers.

She lies down next to **Pete**.

Pete (*angry*) No I wun't, not conifers. I 'ate conifers. That's an insult that is Dot.

Dot (*laughing*) All right, I tek it back.

There is a long pause. **Pete** *sulks.* **Dot** *sunbathes.*

Pete It's always you who 'as the last word.

Dot All right, *you* have it.

Pete Just because you're cleverer than me. I din't want to leave school at thirteen. It were the law.

Dot I *said* I tek it back. I apologised.

Pete Just because you're older.

Dot I used to be. You're an old man now.

Pete I'm thirteen years younger than you!

Dot I know. I wanted you straight off.

Pete *is pleased. He is about to hear a familiar litany.*

Pete Did you? What did you like about me?

Dot The back of your neck. First.

Pete Second?

Dot (*laughing*) You know what.

Pete You din't see that. Not for a week or two.

Dot You were young. Your skin was stretched tight. You 'ad no age on you. You 'ad no wickedness in your face.

Pete It were you that were wicked! It were you that took me cherry!

Dot I know . . . but weren't it lovely?

Pete It were. I'm glad Dot. I would'a bin 'opeless out 'ere without you.

Dot Youd'a managed.

Pete No. No. No. I wouldn't. You would'a done. But I wouldn't. I'd'a chucked miself out the winder like all me mates.

Dot (*loudly*) Spongebacks! That's what your mates were, spongebacks! Take your own life away? Give *them* the satisfaction of seein' you sprawled in a heap with your brains runnin' into each other!

Pete It's 'ard. They couldn't tek it.

Dot Well we can. I don't care how hard it gets. We're a family of two, we look after each other. We're staying on that computer until *Nature* kills us. We get us money tomorrow. Food Pete.

Pete Can I have a tin of beans?

Dot If they're in the shop. You've stopped stroking my legs.

Pete Did you like it?

Dot I did like it.

Pete Shall I stroke you all over, in the sunshine.

Dot Yes.

Pete An' in the wind?

Dot Yes.

Pete An' shall we make a baby?

Dot (*sitting up*) Don't call it that! We can't ever make a baby.

Pete It's just my name for it.

Dot It's a stupid name. Say, 'Shall I make love to you Dot?' Or 'Shall I fuck you Dot?'

Pete I don't like that word! You shouldn't say it.

Dot Shall I make love to you Pete? In the sunshine an' in the wind. Shall I stroke you all over? Shall I hear you breathin' fast and sayin' my name and shoutin' when you come?

Pete You're makin' me big.

Dot Good. I want you big. I want you to fill me up.

They lie face to face.

Blackout.

Scene Three

The Salesman's Office

Lucinda *and* **Ralph** *buy a baby.*

A desk. Two low slung chairs. **Ralph** *and* **Lucinda** *sitting in them.* **Ralph** *squirms about trying to get comfortable.*

Lucinda Ralph, sit still!

Ralph (*raising himself*) Look Luce, I know all about this chair psychology, he'll be up there looking down on us and we'll be flopping about like dying goldfish. So I'll stand.

Ralph *struggles out of his chair.*

Lucinda Ralph, for God's sake, we're here to buy a baby, not to indulge in chit chat about furniture. Sit down!

Alan, *the salesman, enters.*

Alan Alan Cathcart. And you must be Mr and Mrs Darling. How very very nice.

Ralph *and* **Alan** *shake hands.*

Ralph My wife, Mrs Darling.

Alan A Darling indeed. (*He shakes* **Lucinda**'s *hand.*)

Lucinda Please excuse my moist palm.

Ralph She's nervous. Thinks you'll turn us down.

Alan Oh now we can't have that! Please, sit back in your chair! Relax Mrs Darling. Think of me as a friend.

Lucinda I'll try.

Ralph *and* **Lucinda** *sit right back in the low slung chairs.*

Alan I've been looking at your records, and very impressive they are too. Very very sound financially, very very good citizenship report. A *little* heavy on the drinking Ralph. (*He laughs.*) Shows you're human eh? I like a drink myself.

Ralph I work hard.

Alan Very very hard . . . it's all in here. (*Taps file.*) Look, I want to help you, sure. But I've gotta be a hundred per cent certain that our products are going to be *cherished.* That they're truly *wanted.* Don't want you bringing one back do we?

Lucinda We wouldn't be here if we didn't . . . sincerely and wholeheartedly want a baby.

Alan (*cutting in*) 'Course not. Right, so . . . a few questions, OK?

Ralph *takes* **Lucinda**'s *hand.*

Ralph Fire away!

Alan So, you'd really like a baby?

Lucinda Yes.

Ralph Yes, she would.

Alan And you Ralph?

Ralph I'm easy, but she really would like one wouldn't you Luce?

Lucinda I've just *said* yes.

Alan Why Lucinda?

Lucinda Why?

Ralph (*little laugh*) Good question. Answer him Luce.

Lucinda I'd like a baby because I've failed to conceive one of my own: I've not even had the misfortune of a miscarriage.

Ralph My fault. Thin sperm. Luce is in the clear.

Lucinda It hadn't used to bother me much, not having one. I've worked with Ralph, we've built up the business . . .

Alan Which is?

Ralph Drinking straws. Specials . . . cocktails . . . children's parties.

Lucinda I'd be a good mother.

Ralph She would. Maternal! You should have seen her with the dog. You spoon fed her round the clock once, didn't you Luce?

Lucinda *ignores* **Ralph.** *She leans towards* **Alan.**

Lucinda Just lately, recently, I've *longed* for a baby. My arms have felt completely empty.

Ralph Like her brain. (*Laughs.*)

Lucinda Actually I am quite intelligent.

Ralph Luce!

Luce I am, I've kept quiet about it until now. I knew you wouldn't like it. I've had to rein back my vocabulary. Forego the use of multi-syllabled words.

Ralph What she talkin' about?

Lucinda See?

Alan (*he raises his hand*) I do indeed Lucinda. Ralph can you name one advantage of having a baby living with you in your house?

Ralph One advantage?

He stares ahead, whistling between his teeth. Shakes his head. He doesn't know.

Lucinda (*prompting*) In the car you were saying how lovely it would be to buy toys for a little one . . . weren't you?

Ralph (*to* **Alan**) Oh yeah, I love toy shops. Bloody tragedy of life isn't it? That when you're a kid you look in the window . . . wanting something so badly, and you know you'll never have it, 'cos you're skint. Then, soon as, you know, you're grown up and you've got the money: well you can't can you? You can't walk in and buy toys for yourself can you?

Alan You'd enjoy *playing* with a small child then Ralph?

Ralph Oh yeah. I'd put time aside in the day for *that*. An hour at least.

Lucinda And in that hour I shall rest and practice being my own person. In another room.

Alan You've certainly done your homework! Talked it through!

Ralph 'Til dawn. Birdsong. Bags under eyes.

Lucinda We examined our marriage for obvious *and* hidden defects. But we concluded that in spite of certain difficulties, we'd make fantastic parents.

Alan You realise Lucinda that you would have to stop working?

Lucinda Yes, I'm fully conversant with the regulations. Quite frankly it would be a relief to stop working. Sending out invoices for drinking straws is hardly totally fulfilling is it?

Ralph Don't knock the straws Luce. They've given you a good life. Even, dare I say it, a lifestyle. Think about the Trade Exhibitions, you'd miss *them*.

Lucinda I wasn't knocking the straws Ralph. But I think that a baby would be more fulfilling. I'd do a good job. The government would be proud of me. And I wouldn't miss the Trade Exhibitions Ralph. Birmingham, Harrogate, Brighton, Leeds, I've been there, done it. It's time my energy was directed towards something more meaningful. Motherhood.

There is a silence of fifteen seconds.

Alan Why prolong the agony, eh? Yes, we'll sell you a baby.

Lucinda Ralph!

She tries to get out of the chair. **Ralph** *gets up and pulls her free of the chair. They embrace.*

Ralph Luce! Oh my beautiful Lucinda! You're going to be a mummy. (*To* **Alan**.) Thanks!

Alan Do you want a laboratory grown baby, or do you want to give birth yourself?

Lucinda Oh I want to give birth. I want to experience the agony and the joy. I want to come through the ordeal (*Warning.*) and I want Ralph there to see me do it.

Alan Now there's something . . . you may be disappointed . . . but I'm afraid the quota for boys is full for this year.

Ralph (*obviously disappointed*) Oh. So what's left?

Lucinda Girls!

Alan Yes girls. (*Laughing.*) There was a time when one couldn't be so *definite*. But, now there are just the two sexes.

Ralph (*to* **Lucinda**) You don't want to wait? (*To* **Alan**.) How long for a boy?

Alan Next January.

Ralph You don't want to wait Luce? I'd set my heart on a boy. A lad, a son.

Lucinda No. A girl would be lovely. (*Pause.*) She would have to be pretty.

Alan All our girls are pretty.

Ralph We'll have a beautiful one. A head turner, I'll pay extra.

Lucinda She must have a good brain.

Ralph Not too good. Don't want her looking down on her old mum and dad. But bright enough to pass her exams.

Lucinda We're hoping she'll make it to Grade Two.

Alan I just missed getting a Two. Had a distant relation with a criminal record. Shoplifting, a tin of pilchards.

Lucinda Oh what a shame, just think, if it wasn't for a tin of pilchards you could be living in the Home Counties. Oh fate is vile.

Ralph (*to* **Alan**) Is your section the same as ours, Watford Gap to Scotch Corner?

Alan Yes, I can holiday in the Cairngorms or Penzance.

Ralph Same us us! What a very small world we live in.

Lucinda A staggering coincidence. Can we get back to choosing our daughter?

Alan There are five Grade Three females to choose from.

Ralph Just show us the blondes!

Lucinda With the blue eyes, five foot six – any bigger and there could be trouble in the years to come, with men.

On a screen appears a picture of a blonde blue-eyed child of two.

Ralph She's a little cracker!

Lucinda A sweetheart. Is there another one?

On the screen appears a picture of a less attractive two year old.

Lucinda Oh it's the first one, isn't it Ralph?

Ralph She'll do for me. Numero uno.

Alan Of course she'll inherit some of yours and your wife's features and characteristics as well, we're not breeding a society of clones here.

They all laugh.

Ralph So, when will you do the business?

Alan According to your wife's menstrual cycle, the next suitable day would be Thursday at 11.30, and you can have the simple medical procedure or something more celebratory.

Ralph Such as?

Alan Oh you know, balloons, party poppers. Timed to coincide with the moment that the sperm meets the ovum.

Ralph What do you think Luce? Fancy a little party next Thursday?

Lucinda We ought to mark the occasion. Yes, a few party poppers.

Ralph And champagne, I'll supply the straws.

Alan And will you want a video recording of the ceremony? Something to treasure in the years ahead?

Lucinda No! I prefer to keep my private parts, private.

Ralph Oh well, in that case . . .

Lucinda I don't want a baby on the cheap Ralph. What will she think if she finds out she was 20% off?

Alan *writes out the invoice.*

Ralph She'll think it was good business practice. (*To* **Alan**.) Yeah, give us the discount. (*To* **Lucinda**.) A video star eh Luce? Make sure you get your legs waxed.

Alan Right, so, if you can give me a cheque, made out to Government Babies Ltd.

Ralph Sure, sure, is there VAT on babies?

Scene Four

The **Orderly** *changes the Salesman's Office into the venue for the Conception Ceremony.*

She talks to the audience.

Orderly I keep thinking it's Friday. I'm off this weekend, going to see my mum, she's only got five months to go. Three days, five months. She's being difficult though, she says they'll have to come and get her, she won't do it herself. I'm hoping she'll change her mind, it could reflect badly on me. She doesn't see why she should have to go at all. She says she's fit and well and good for another twenty years. She thinks she's invincible. The invincible woman. I've said to her, 'What's the point of living on after seventy years? You're not working, you're not generating wealth, your brain will go, your body will fall apart. It's unpatriotic. You'll be a parasite.' She's still living in the old days when people died all over the place – on holiday, in the car, in shops. It was inconvenient and it caused a lot of disruption. People having days off work for funerals and rushing about with death certificates. I said, 'Mum you're being selfish – it's a tiny injection and then a long sleep. You deserve it, you've worked hard' – but she wouldn't listen. I hope she'll be in, she sometimes goes off at the weekends – painting with an easel she found on a rubbish tip. She walks miles with this easel thing under her arm. She's a terrible embarrassment to me. And you know what she paints? The countryside! (*She laughs.*) Don't ask me why. She's got all these little *pictures* up on the walls in her room. It's a sign of senility. I mean there are professionals whose job it is to paint pictures. *She* doesn't need to do it. I'm surprised she's got away with it for so long. And now this stubborn attitude she's taking towards Death Day. (*Determined.*) Well she'll have to go along with it. I've booked a day off for it and I can't go chopping and changing – it's on the computer now, so that's final. It'll be a relief for me when she's gone. I can concentrate on my work. At the moment I'm a bag of nerves, wondering what the daft old bat will do next. If it gets out about the pictures . . .

She takes a card out of her pocket and checks the room.

Lucinda Darling. Husband Ralph. Government Section Three. Secular, religious and video ceremony. (*She shouts.*) Ready! Wheel 'em in. Ten seconds!

She stands and picks her teeth with the edge of the card.

I hope she'll be in.

Scene Five

The Fertilisation Ceremony

A quasi-religious setting with a **Priest**. **Alan** *is present with* **Ralph** *and* **Lucinda**. *There is an altar-like structure.*

Alan (*to* Priest) Before we start sweetheart, can you manage a smile now and then, to the camera?

Priest This is a religious ceremony Mr Cathcart.

Alan (*cutting in*) And haven't you got a spot of lipstick . . .?

Priest I don't wear lipstick.

Alan You'll be sorry when you see the video. How old are you?

Priest I'm in my forties.

Alan I'd have said ten years older. Spot of lipstick eh? To give the illusion of youth? (*He snaps his fingers.*)

The **Orderly** *applies lipstick to the* **Priest**.

Alan 'Mazing difference. Another woman. Right, you can start now. Forget about the camera, but remember to smile. We're flogging babies here, not headache pills.

Priest I wasn't told that I was officiating at a Sales Promotion Mr Cathcart. I'm afraid I can't go ahead (*Pause.*) at least not until you agree to increase my fee, and what about residuals?

Alan All right, I'll talk to your agent. You're with Binky Brown Associates aren't you?

Priest For the moment, but the work he's been getting me lately . . .

Alan Time to go sweethearts. First positions everyone. Cheer up Lucinda. Right video on and, go!

Priest Come forward Lucinda. (**Lucinda** *goes forward.*) Lucinda, repeat after me: 'With the fertile egg I do bear in my womb I do offer my life, my thoughts, my peace of mind. My work.'

Lucinda *repeats the words.*

Priest Hast thou the egg?

Lucinda I have.

Lucinda *passes an egg to the* **Priest** *who breaks it into a chalice.*

Priest Come forward Ralph. (**Ralph** *comes forward.*) Repeat after me the following words: 'With this seed I do give life in the knowledge that in so doing I offer the most precious of gifts.'

Ralph *repeats the words.*

Priest Hast thou thy seed?

Ralph I have.

*The **Priest** takes a packet of seed from **Ralph** and puts the seed into the chalice.*

Priest Who does deign to join together this egg and this seed?

Alan *steps forward.*

Alan I do, being a representative of the government.

Priest Hast thou the catalyst?

Alan I have.

*He produces a test tube from his inside pocket. The **Priest** takes both test tubes and empties the contents into the chalice. She takes a glass rod and stirs the contents.*

Priest As I stir this egg, this seed and this sperm I make three wishes: The first is that the child be obedient; the second is that the child be worthy; the third is that the child shall respect the State which ultimately gives it life.

Priest Now join hands.

Alan, Lucinda *and* **Ralph** *join hands, the* **Priest** *blesses them and raises the chalice above their heads. She then offers the chalice to them. They 'drink' the contents.* The **Priest** *intones:*

. . . Oh beloved Government who art so mighty and so strong. Bless these your children, Lucinda and Ralph and their unborn child. Keep this little family prosperous and healthy and sensible of their obligation to maintain the purity of their lineage. o-u-r Government.

Priest We will now sing 'There's a friend for little children'.

Everyone sings. **Lucinda** *is led to the altar by the* **Priest**. *She lies down. The cloth is put over her belly. The chalice is put on the altar. The* **Priest** *leaves still singing.* **Ralph** *stands to one side of the stage. He lights a cigar. He is nervous.*

Lucinda Ralph I'm frightened. Will it hurt?

Ralph Quiet Lucinda! You're in church. Lie down like a good girl.

Alan *turns his back to the audience and in the manner of a magician changes into top hat, glittering waistcoat and bow tie. He carries a magician's stick.*

Alan Hello there, and welcome to the secular ceremony. I'm Sales Director of Government Babies Ltd and this (*He extends his arm.*) is my lovely assistant, orderly Meadowcroft.

The **Orderly** *enters, dressed as a magician's assistant. She dips and smirks, then goes to work arranging a device over* **Lucinda**'s *belly. She puts a long syringe in place. As she works* **Alan** *continues his patter.*

May I say what an honour and a privilege it is for me to be officiating on this day, at this hour, and indeed, at the very minute, no, *moment* of conception. Ralph . . . Lucinda.

He extends his hands towards **Ralph** *and* **Lucinda.**

I know you're goin' to make great parents. Just a little about these two fine people. First, Ralph. Ralph Darling is a self-made man. Born in Brighton in humble circumstances, he was ill-educated, lacking capital, and he had Socialist parents.

Ralph *looks alarmed.*

Despite these handicaps, Ralph, by dint of an eighteen hour day, and by showing qualities of ruthlessness and ambition, managed to make it into Section Three. What's it like up there in Section Three Ralph?

Ralph (*smiling*) Mega good.

Alan Indeed, mega good. Ralph first served his government in the Army where he distinguished himself many times, being instrumental in the de-unionising of many powerful industries. For this he was awarded Class Three status.

Ralph *spreads his hands modestly.*

. . . After leaving the Army Ralph met and married his delicious wife, Lucinda. In Ralph's own words, 'I saw her, I wanted her, I got her'. Lucinda Minehead, as she was then, was swept overboard by Ralph's overpowering personality, and one year after their first meeting, at an indoor shooting range, their union was sanctified by our government. From the start theirs was an ecstatic marriage. However, (*He drops his voice, false lump in the throat.*) they were not blessed with the child they longed for. Ralph shed many secret tears, as did Lucinda, but today they are to conceive that child!

He looks at his watch, the lights fade apart from the spotlit altar. Drum roll.

Do you believe in babies? If you do, keep very very quiet, and very very still.

He stills the audience. The **Orderly** *presses the syringe, the contents glow in the dark.*

Conception! Ralph and Lucinda have a baby!

Balloons drop. **Ralph** *catches one and gives it to* **Lucinda.**

Music 'Ten Tiny Fingers, Ten Tiny Toes'.

The **Orderly** *sings and tap dances her way around the stage. After one chorus she stops and turns to the audience.*

Orderly Are you thinking of having a baby? If you are, why not go one better and add that extra ingredient; Government sperm? Give your baby that authority, that character, that unmistakable something that proclaims, 'My baby's a Government baby'.

Government babies are the best. Quiet, docile and sleeping through the night at three weeks. Faddy eaters? Forget it? Tantrums at the checkout? A thing of the past. Rude and rebellious during the teenage years. You must be joking! Not with a Government baby. They come in many colourways apart from black, and are fully guaranteed for seventy years. Go on, make your baby a Government baby.

Music – she sings 'Ten Tiny Fingers, Ten Tiny Toes'. **Alan** *joins in with the harmony, they tap dance at the very front of the stage.*

Lucinda *sits on the altar clutching a balloon, she is uncomfortable and forgotten by everyone.*

Scene Six

The Wilderness, Derbyshire

Winter. A room in a tower block. Very few furnishings, everything was originally something else. The light is very dim.

Dot *and* **Pete** *are asleep in a makeshift bed. They are dressed in rags and covered in rags and old coats. A ragged curtain covers a picture window which shows a snow covered ridge, and, in the distance, moorland.*

A **Police Officer***, breathless from climbing the stairs, pushes the door open. She adjusts her eyesight to the dim light then switches the light switch on, but there is no light working in the room.*

Police Officer Dorothy Bird?

The bedclothes move.

(*Louder.*) Dorothy Bird?

Pete *stirs, sits up in bed. The* **Police Officer** *releases her automatic rifle from its shoulder holster.*

Pete (*pleading*) Don't!

Police Officer (*using the gun to draw back the curtain*) Is that your wife?

Pete Yes.

Police Officer Dorothy Bird?

Pete Yes.

Dorothy *sits up in alarm.* **Pete** *puts his arm round her.*

Police Officer Stand up!

Pete *gets out of bed.*

Police Officer Not you! Her.

Dot *gets up and stands by the bed. She pulls the rags over her belly.*

Police Officer Pull your . . . clothes away from your belly.

Dot (*looking at* **Pete**) They know.

She pulls her clothes away. She is about six months pregnant.

Police Officer Dorothy Bird of room 109 Ridley Tower, Section Five, Axley Edge, Derbyshire. I charge you with being unlawfully pregnant.

Dot I had my tubes tied sixteen years ago. It weren't my fault.

Pete It just happened.

Police Officer You should have reported your first missed period. You know that don't you? Don't you?

Dot Yes.

Police Officer So why didn't you?

Dot We wanted a baby.

Police Officer I see, you wanted to share your life with a child did you? Give it the benefit of your education. Share the material advantages of your lovely home, give it everything you never had?

Dot *and* **Pete** *hang their heads.*

Police Officer They don't want Section Five's breeding that is why there is a law. A Government Law forbidding it.

Pete I'm sorry.

Dorothy I'm not. It's not asking much is it to have a baby? We've got nowt else.

Police Officer (*walking to window, looking out*) On the contrary Mrs Bird, you've got a great deal. Fresh air, magnificent views, is that Congleton there in the distance?

Pete Dunno.

Police Officer Silence, the cry of birds, the clouds passing. Breathtaking.

Dot Fetching the water from the river.

Police Officer Advantageous for the vasco cardio system. Put your clothes on Mrs Bird.

Dot They're on.

Police Officer I see, these are they, are they?

Dot Yes. (*Pause.*) I don't see how you can do your job.

Police Officer You couldn't do it?

Dot No, I couldn't. I don't see how any woman could.

Police Officer I'm not a woman. I'm a police officer. There are only two kinds of people in my world. Police officers and civilians.

Dot You're a woman!

Police Officer I'm a police officer! Senior Police Officer, in charge of the Baby Squad.

Dot You can't enjoy it.

Police Officer It gets me out.

Dot Is that gun loaded?

Police Officer Of course it's loaded. And you may be surprised if I told you how many times I've used it.

Dot On pregnant women?

Police Officer On law-breakers.

Dot Do you shoot them through the belly? Do you?

Police Officer I shoot if my own life is threatened. Some of the women go, quite literally, mad.

Pete Don't lose your temper Dot. Don't go mad.

Dot It's all right love, I won't.

Dot *goes to* **Pete**.

Pete Where's she going?

Police Officer To the town. How long is it since you went to the town Mrs Bird?

Dot Since we were classified weren't it Pete?

Pete Long while ago, can't remember. Is it Buxton you're going to?

Police Officer Yes, Buxton.

Pete Can I come?

Police Officer No, Mr Bird. You stay here and admire the view. You're a country man, would you say it was going to snow?

Pete Dunno, radio's broke.

Dot (*to* **Pete**) I've hidden a great heap of firewood by the hanging rock, don't go mad with it will you? Eke it out.

Pete Will they take the baby off you Dot?

Dot I 'ope not. Now don't forget to fetch the water before dark will you?

Pete No. Firewood and water. Owt else?

Dot *looks around the room, giving it a last check.*

Dot Not that I can think of.

The **Police Officer** *is looking at a small picture frame.*

Police Officer And who are these laughing boyos then?

Pete (*proud*) That's me an' my mates. It was took on our first day at work.

Police Officer So you have worked?

Dot (*indignantly*) He's had *three* jobs.

Pete Concrete post handler. Grass cutter and motorway maintenance. First job I were 14, that were for Manpower Services. Second job I were 15 that were for a Council Scheme. Third job I were 16 that were called Job Training. (*Pause.*) Then I were nowt. (*Pause.*) Then I were sent to live 'ere.

Police Officer (*to* **Dot**) Have you got a toothbrush?

Dot No.

Police Officer A handbag?

Dot No.

Police Officer Say goodbye.

She turns her back to allow them privacy. **Dot** *and* **Pete** *clutch each other passionately. It is obvious they care for and need each other.*

Scene Seven

The countryside, Derbyshire

The **Orderly** *is looking at a painting on an easel. She is sitting on a tattered canvas fold up stool. There is a picture of clouds on the easel.*

Orderly It's signed. Susan Louise Meadowcroft. Clouds. Her paints ran out. She couldn't squeeze any more out of the tubes. Then she died. Natural causes. Here. It was typical! She couldn't die like everybody else. Not her. There'll be repercussions. I could lose status because of this. (*Pause.*) The clothes she was wearing! OK, she'd been out in the weather, but even so, she looked like a Class Five. And now I've got to lug all this rubbish back. Susan Louise Meadowcroft. She had nothing in her stomach but wild garlic and an unidentifiable fish. I *gave* her money for food! She had a ration book! There were tins in her room! She'd been round the neighbours asking for paint! Desperate for it! Begging! Nobody had any. (*Contemptuously.*) Clouds! Why would anybody want to paint them? They're up there for real every day – if you really wanted to look at them. (*She gathers up the easel and chair.*) And why die here? She must have known it belongs to the Ministry of Defence, she must have seen the signs. She had no right to be here. (*She looks up, looking at the clouds.*) They are lovely, when you really look at them. But who's got the time?

Scene Eight.

Buxton maternity unit.

A two-bedded room in a modern maternity unit. **Dot** *is lying on her bed. She is heavily pregnant. She has no flowers or cards on her bedside locker.* **Lucinda** *is standing by her bed, which is opposite* **Dot***'s. She is glamorous in her pregnancy, lace negligée, fluffy mules, full make-up.*

Lucinda So Zanna told Steve that Amanda was Kurt's baby and Steve told Zanna that he had a love child in Barbados. Are you following?

Dot Sort of.

Lucinda You don't look very interested.

Dot I don't know any of these people do I?

Lucinda I don't *know* them.

Dot You're talking about them as if you do.

Lucinda They're characters, on television.

Dot I haven't got a television.

Lucinda (*seriously*) Do you live in a cave?

Dot (*laughing*) No.

Lucinda Some Section Fives do. Ralph told me.

Dot So what did Zanna do about this love child?

Lucinda She kidnapped it, a sweet little boy called Phoenix. She hired a microlight plane and swooped down (*Pause.*) . . . it's on now. It's so frustrating. I've never missed an episode.

Dot Perhaps your husband will bring one in.

Lucinda Telly's aren't allowed. I've been through all that.

The **Orderly** *enters with a florists arrangement of real flowers in a basket. She looks at* **Dot**, **Dot** *indicates wearily that the flowers must be for* **Lucinda.**

Dot They won't be for me.

Lucinda *turns her head and acknowledges the flowers. She touches them, she recoils.*

Lucinda Ugh! What are they made of exactly?

Orderly I don't know exactly, I'm not a Biochemist am I? I have an uncomplicated job. I fetch and I carry. (*Pause.*) Madam.

Lucinda (*hastily*) That *madam* was too long in coming (*Half beat.*) again.

Orderly These flowers madam are real, they grew in the ground.

Somebody planted the seeds, watered the seedlings, and then, when the flowers were considered tall enough to stand up to the rigours of bouquet life they were torn from the earth and arranged as you see (*Pause.*) madam.

Lucinda I don't like real flowers. They die.

Orderly Yes, it's an unfortunate tendency shared by all living things.

The **Orderly** *leaves.*

Dot There's freesias in there somewhere, I can smell them. I nearly had freesias at my wedding.

Lucinda Which wedding?

Dot I've only had the one. It din't work out, I'm glad now. Then I met Pete and I fell for him an' 'e fell for me.

Lucinda Is he good looking?

Dot 'E's strong, and 'e's kind. I don't know if 'e's good lookin'. 'E can't read, but I taught him to write his name. He can *do* things, he can mackle things together. He made the fireplace in our flat. We can burn wood now and it costs us nowt. When he were sixteen 'e won a trophy. A silver trowel, for being the best bricklayer. 'E put it on the wall the day we moved in to the flat. 'E were so proud of it. We went out to the shop, come back and some bugger 'ad broke in an' took it. I *told* him to hide it somewhere, I went mad at him. Then I went round all the flats in the block looking for this silver trowel. (*Pause.*) There's 192 flats in our block.

Lucinda You didn't find it, this trowel thing?

Dot No. But when I come back 'e said, 'Now I know you love me Dot'.

Lucinda How quaint.

Dot It's not quaint, I've never really loved anybody else, 'cept Pete, and nobody else has ever loved me.

Lucinda How old were you when you let yourself go?

Dot *gets out of bed.*

Dot I don't know, have I then?

Lucinda We're the same age Dorothy, yet look at the difference between us. It's astounding, you can't compare.

Dot You're a Class Three though aren't you? You've had a very easy life.

Lucinda Easy! My body and my home are open to inspection at any hour of the day and night. A ragged finger nail, a lump of hard skin, a dusty mantelpiece and I lose points. I can never relax, never. I'm on full alert, every nerve and sinew tensed . . . waiting.

Dot There's an ex-Class Three in our block.

Lucinda Poor wretched woman. It must be hell for her. Why was she demoted?

Dot The inspectors came round at three o'clock in the morning . . .

Lucinda They do! They do!

Dot They found a week's ironing hidden at the back of her wardrobe.

Lucinda Serves her right. I mean all Class Three's are issued with machines . . .

Dot Her drains were blocked an' all.

Lucinda Don't say 'an all' Dorothy, I'm very impressionable, I might start saying it, then where would I be?

Dot Moving into our section that's where. (*She laughs.*)

Lucinda Don't even joke about it. Public Building, it's a recurring nightmare of mine. How do you stand living out there, in the wilderness?

Dot I've forgotten there's owt else.

Lucinda Don't say 'owt'! I don't know why I'm in here with you, do you know why?

Dot No.

Lucinda We've got nothing in common have we?

Dot We're both havin' babies.

Lucinda (*snorts contemptuously*) We're galaxies apart . . . galaxies. There's an unpleasant odour emanating from these things. (*She throws the flowers into a very large rubbish bin.*)

Dot Don't! You don't even know who they're from . . .

Lucinda I don't wish to know a person who sends reminders of death through the post.

Dot Death?

Lucinda Real things die. (*She crushes the flowers in the bin with her feet.*)

Dot You're getting emotional.

Lucinda Yes I am. I've felt emotional all day. (*She paces up and down.*) It's being in here with you! Why me? Why are we sharing facilities? Have I been downgraded, or have you been upgraded? I'm entitled to know.

Dot Ask them.

Lucinda I'm too ashamed to ask. I prefer to pull a thin veil over present reality. I'm terrified of catching your dialect.

Dot I'll keep me gob shut then. (*She turns laboriously towards the audience, she is upset.*)

Lucinda I've done everything that was asked of me. I stayed at home for the past nine months. I practiced all the female arts. I've got certificates for freezer maintenance and microwave cookery. I've got all the tradesmen on floppy disc. What have I done wrong? Why am I sharing a room with you? You're Class Five and I'm a Government woman, I'm entitled to give birth amongst my own kind, who knows what influences will . . .

The **Orderly** *brings in two trays, and wordlessly bangs them onto the bed trolleys.*

Lucinda Are you busy?

Orderly Yes. (*She goes out, shutting the door. She returns instantly.*) Madam.

Lucinda (*harshly*) Stop there.

The **Orderly** *stops.*

You know of course that I'm a Government woman?

Orderly Yes.

Lucinda And that Dorothy there is a Class Five unskilled, uneducated?

Orderly Yes.

Lucinda Why are we sharing the same room?

Orderly Computer error.

Lucinda (*smiling*) There! I knew it!

Orderly That's what I was told to tell you if you asked.

Dot Who by?

Lucinda *By whom*, Dorothy! I shall be lucky to get out of here with my grammar intact.

Orderly By Mister Crudwell.

Lucinda But my consultant is Mr Fernie.

Orderly Not any more he's not, Mister Crudwell is looking after you now.

Lucinda Since when?

Orderly Since they found out that your baby's got a defect.

Lucinda *lets out a long wail, she clutches her baby.*

Dot (*to* **Orderly**) You cruel bastard.

Orderly As I said, I'm busy. (*She goes out.*)

Dot (*approaching* **Lucinda**) Lucinda.

Lucinda It can't have a defect. I've got a guarantee – on paper. A perfect baby: blonde, blue eyes, 5 foot 6 inches at maturity. There's a mistake, it's your baby that's got the defect. Government women give birth to Government approved babies!

Dot It might not be much.

Lucinda It has to be perfect Dorothy!

Dot I know.

Lucinda It's impossible, my womb has been investigated by experts. I've had state of the art technology photographing my reproductive organs since conception.

Crudwell *enters. He is 33, he is wearing a morning coat and striped trousers etc. He is affable, smiles a lot. He stands and looks at the two women.*

Crudwell (*to* **Lucinda**) It's you I've come to see isn't it? Mrs Darling?

Lucinda I don't know. Who are you? You look like a wedding guest.

Crudwell Not a guest Mrs Darling. The best man. (*He laughs.*) I'm your consultant, Mr Crudwell.

Lucinda Mr Fernie wears a white coat.

Crudwell Ah, it's some years since I attended a birth Mrs Darling. Do you shop in a hypermarket Mrs Darling?

Lucinda Yes of course, the one reserved for Government women.

Crudwell Whilst in there, browsing amongst the merchandise, have you heard the phrase 'So and so, come to Quality Control' resounding from the tannoy?

Lucinda Yes.

Crudwell Well that's my job here, quality controller. Of course I'm not interested in wrinkled carrots or dubious joints of pork, but I am responsible for maintaining standards.

Lucinda I was informed only a moment ago that the child I am carrying has a defect.

Crudwell Yes, that is, sadly, the case.

Lucinda What is the nature of the defect?

Crudwell She lacks a toe.

Lucinda A toe?

Crudwell Specifically the little toe on the right foot. Where her little piggy should be is a gap, a vacuum.

Dot *shows her relief.*

Lucinda Will she be able to walk?

Crudwell Oh yes. But you won't ever see her walk. When she is born she will be taken away immediately, and she will die in her sleep.

Lucinda No!

Crudwell Her life will consist of a few short minutes. She will feel no pain, no fear, she won't even be aware that she once existed.

Dot No!

Crudwell Yes Mrs Bird! (*To* **Lucinda**.) I've had the decency, in spite of the distress it *always* causes me, to come and inform you of our intentions. Now, I ask you to remember that you are a Grade Three woman, certain things are expected of you, dignity in the face of difficulty is one.

Lucinda Could I please keep the baby sir? I'm willing to drop a grade. I could live a Grade Four life. Leeds and its environs is quite a pleasant place.

Crudwell The latest regulations apply to all grades. Of course Grade Fives are not allowed to breed at all.

He looks at **Dot**, *she stares back at him. She would like to shout and scream, but daren't.*

Dot You won't take mine off me.

Crudwell (*brightly*) We have made other arrangements for your child. A boy, a perfectly healthy boy. Ten tiny fingers, ten tiny toes. Everything in its place. Quite an exceptional child. We are very interested in him.

Dot His name is Peter.

Crudwell Is it? I'll remember that. Peter Bird.

Lucinda No, I'm afraid you don't understand, I don't mind about the toe. What's a missing toe? She'll have nine others to compensate for the lack of one. I must keep her, I've carried her around for nine months and I've grown rather fond of her, in fact very fond. And we've paid a great deal of money for this baby. We've liquidised a share portfolio to pay for her nursery. The decorator's bill alone! Blush pink walls, white ceiling and a lilac dado. We've bought the furniture: a wicker basket lined in hand made lace. A patchwork quilt which took six women five months to complete. A changing mat on a table of a suitable height to prevent back injury. An Edwardian nursing chair. Her clothes are waiting for her! They're in an old sea captain's chest. My husband has ordered six cases of genuine Australian champagne from an ex-directory wholesaler, Freephone 001122. I've enrolled for a part-time degree in child nutrition – she won't be allowed to eat sugar or salt. I will train her palette – I was 25 before I enjoyed a quail's egg.

Crudwell Now stop it.

Lucinda She's going to the best playgroup in Greater Manchester. Ralph knows influential people. I've ordered a sand-pit. I've chosen her name. Her pram cover is hand embroidered, copied from the one Zanna's mother gave her for Phoenix in *Flippers Retreat*. The women stitching it went blind – that's how small the stitches are. I've chosen her friends! I've *pored* over genealogical text books. I know who she's going to marry! His name is Crispin Browne-Hogg and he's two and a half years old and he's going to be a plastic surgeon. We've planned a huge party for next Saturday – my deep freeze is packed to the gills with frozen canapes – look! Look! Frostbite! So you see don't you Mr Crudwell, that you cannot take my daughter away and kill her, because of all the aforementioned arrangements?

Crudwell It is unfortunate Mrs Darling, tragic even. But no child of Government parents can be born with the slightest defect. The line must be drawn. We are aiming for perfection in our governing class. Healthy, wealthy and wise. I am very *cross* that you've been allowed to go the full term. Much easier to have aborted the child in the early months. Why this missing toe was not noted before now . . .

Lucinda Yes it *is* tragic. I'm in the middle of a tragic situation, I can feel emotions quite foreign to me snarling at the back of my throat. (*She snarls.*) I want her. I want my baby. I'll give you anything! Money? I've got money . . . I've got a platinum card in my bag. Take as much as you need.

Crudwell No.

Lucinda Sex, do you want sex? You can have *me*. (*She slips her negligée off revealing her arms and shoulders.*)

Crudwell (*with disgust*) No! Adjust your clothing Mrs Darling please!

Lucinda All right we'll arm wrestle for her, I'm stronger than you think. (*She grasps his hand. She grunts and strains.*)

Lucinda I'm winning, I'm winning, I'm going to win.

Crudwell *forces her arm down, she lays her head on her knees.*

Lucinda It's such a very tiny thing, easy to miss.

Dot It's not as though it's a leg or a brain . . .

Crudwell I'm forbidden to breed myself. Eczema runs in the family. (*To* **Lucinda**.) It was nice to meet you, if you feel the need of pre-bereavement counselling, get in touch. Crudwell, Research and Development. Just down the corridor.

Door opens and he exits after flashing a lovely smile at the two women.

The **Orderly** *puts her head round the door.*

Orderly Your husband's here, he knows about the toe, lack of.

Lucinda Who told him?

Orderly I did.

Lucinda How did he take it?

Orderly He asked for his money back.

Lucinda Where is he now?

Orderly He's on the phone to the Consumer Complaints Bureau. He's a very unpleasant man isn't he?

Lucinda He's a businessman, his first reaction is bound to be a financial one. His second will be the legal aspects, only then will he give way to his own private grief.

Orderly He's coming. I'm off.

Lucinda *arranges herself back on the pillows. She dabs at her eyes with a lace handkerchief.* **Ralph** *bursts in.*

Ralph There's nothing on my side of the family that points to missing extremities, is there on yours? Since Magna Carta my family has had its full complement of toes.

Lucinda How can you possibly know? Have you exhumed their bodies?

Ralph Yes, yes, I have, with my own bare hands. I found nothing untoward.

Lucinda Stop telling lies Ralph, you haven't had time for exhumations.

Ralph OK, OK, so I exaggerated slightly, but I'm in the clear, it didn't get its missing toe from me. Understood Lucinda?

Lucinda (*sticking feet out of bed*) Count! . . . Count! Take an inventory! Count!

Ralph It's your father then, you told me once he never took his shoes off. One of your earliest recollections was of him walking on the beach at Polperro wearing ox-blood brogues and bathing trunks wasn't it?

Lucinda Ralph I don't care if she hasn't got ten toes. I've always thought ten was an extravagance, an unnecessary waste of flesh and tissue . . .

Ralph It's deformed! The kid's deformed!

Lucinda All it means is that some of her bootees will have to be taken in. It'll save me work, one less toenail to cut.

Ralph I'll get the money back and I'll buy you another. A boy.

Ralph junior. He can inherit the straws Luce. 'Darling and Son', in black paint on a white board. You'll be stunned with pride one day. Forget about that mutated little cow you've got in your belly Luce.

Pause. **Lucinda** *turns on her back, crying.* **Ralph** *turns to* **Dot.**

Ralph Is your kid damaged or deformed?

Dot No.

Ralph Boy or girl?

Dot Boy.

Ralph Want to sell him?

Dot No.

Ralph I could ask your husband.

Dot He'd say no an' all.

Ralph Where'd you live?

Dot Axley Edge.

Ralph Section Five! In here with my wife?

Lucinda She's a human being.

Ralph Barely, Lucinda. (*He goes to* **Lucinda**.) I'll be back in the morning.

Lucinda In for the kill.

Ralph *leaves.*

Scene Nine

The tower block

Pete's *and* **Dot**'s *room.* **Pete** *putting firewood on the small grate. He looks into the flames.*

Pete I done like you said, I've been a good boy, careful with the wood, still got some and you been gone a long time. When you coming home Dot? (*Pause.*) A bloke on the fifteenth floor told me there's a job goin'. I don't know where but sounds all right eh? A chance anyway. He's goin' to try and find out – details – that sort of thing. I don't know who this bloke is. But, he was nice, you'd have taken a shine like I did. He looked all right. I an't been to see you

Dot 'cos I don't know where you are. I went up to the roof last
night, the wind nearly 'ad me. I tried to see Buxton then I 'ad to
stop lookin' 'cos my eyes froze up. I 'ope you'll come back soon,
'specially now there's the chance of this job. I don't know his name,
but I gave 'im mine. Pete Bird I said, that's my name. I told 'im
which room it was. He didn't write it down. Will he remember or 'as
'e already forgot?

Pete *gets up from the fire. He goes and stands in front of the picture on the
wall. As he speaks he points to the youths in the picture.*

. . . Barry, 'e were a big 'un. 'E could carry a post on 'is own. Glen,
'e were a black boy, 'is mam used to wrap 'is sandwiches dead tidy
like she'd bought 'em in a shop. Martin, 'e left. Tony, 'e were a
blabber mouth, always yakkin', 'e told lies an' all. Then me, Pete
Bird, I were a good worker, never lost a minute. Allus turned up
even when it were snowin'. My work were more important to me
that owt else. It weren't just work, it were helpin'.

Come back 'ome Dot. I ain't feeling right. Sommat's missin'. It's
like when me mum died, I'm not that fussed about the baby if the
truth's known, I only want it 'cos you want it. We've done without
it, we've got by. Come 'ome Dot.

He goes to the firewood, breaks a stick viciously then places one piece on the fire.

So, it's good news about this job, eh?

Ralph's *voice is heard outside.*

Pete *is agitated, frightened, nobody ever calls unannounced.*

Ralph Mr Bird?

Pete *stands at the door wringing his hands, afraid.*

Pete Yes.

Ralph (*outside*) I want a word.

Pete Why?

Ralph (*pushing the door open. Puts his head round the door*) I'm Ralph
Darling, have you got time for a little chat? A conversation?

Pete What about?

Ralph You're not . . . busy?

Pete No.

Ralph I can come in then?

Pete Yes.

Ralph *steps into the room. He is dressed in warm clothes.*

Ralph Took me ten minutes to walk up.

Pete The lift's broke.

Ralph Lights are out on the stairs.

Pete I know.

Ralph You could break your neck. (*Pause.*) Bloody cold in here.

Pete There's a fire.

Pete *points to the fire.* **Ralph** *walks to the fire, crouches in front of it.*

Ralph You should put some more wood on.

Pete I 'ave to be careful.

Ralph (*putting sticks on fire*) Careful . . . where did careful get anybody? Nowhere. Hypothermia. You look like you've got it now, no offence but you do. Let me feel your hand.

Pete *reluctantly holds out his hand.* **Ralph** *touches his hand.*

Ralph Freezing, you're a corpse. Put some more clothes on.

Pete *takes a coat off the bed and puts it on while* **Ralph** *is speaking.*

Ralph First time I've been to a Class Five Section. I feared for my suspension Mr Bird, I really did. That road is one big pothole. Thank God for four wheel drive, that's what I say. Think it'll be all right down there? The hub caps, kids won't scratch it?

Ralph *crosses to the window, looks down.*

Pete There ain't no kids.

Ralph (*relieved*) 'Course. What a view! You're very lucky to have this every day. You know we take it for granted don't we, the English countryside? There it is day in, day out, unregarded, forgotten. We drive past it in our cars. You're sure it'll be all right, the car?

Pete Nobody wun't dare touch it.

Ralph Respect for property, now that's a rare thing. I'm a businessman Mr Bird, petty pilfering is the bane of my life. D'you know my employees smuggle drinking straws out of my plant despite the presence of a hundred and fifty thousand K's worth of security cameras?

Pete (*joyfully*) You've come about the job! To tell you the truth I weren't sure about that bloke – whether 'e was 'avin' me on. I din't think you'd come 'ere. I were expectin' to come to you.

Ralph (*baffled*) The job?

Pete That bloke on the fifteenth floor! What sort of job is it?

Ralph I manufacture drinking straws. 'Darlings'? Television advertising slogan, 'Suck up Darlings'?

Pete I think I *might* 'ave 'eard of it. But we don't go in for 'em.

Ralph Cocktails and soft drinks not to your taste?

Pete No offence. It wouldn't stop me havin' a job wi' you would it?

Ralph No, not necessarily. It's a bit bare in here. You having cash flow problems?

Pete Beg your pardon?

Ralph How long is it since you worked Mr Bird?

Pete 'Bout ten year.

Ralph And how desperate are you for a job?

Pete I'm very desperate.

Ralph You'd do anything for a job?

Pete I wouldn't murder no one.

Ralph *laughs.*

Ralph My wife, Lucinda, and your wife, Dot, are sharing a room in hospital, now how's that for a coincidence?

Pete (*laughing*) I can't hardly believe it. How's Dot? Has she had the baby?

Ralph Dot is blooming, and the baby's due this morning. At noon.

Pete What's the time now?

Ralph A quarter to eight.

Pete Does Dot know you've come 'ere?

Ralph No, it's a surprise. I've come to take you to the hospital, to see her. I've got your pass, twenty four hours.

Ralph *hands* **Pete** *a slip of paper,* **Pete** *looks at it.*

Pete I can't read. Thank you Mr Darling. I feel like me 'ead's going to explode. First the job, then seeing Dot . . . Is she in the big town?

Ralph She's in Buxton Maternity Unit.

Pete *starts to cry.*

Ralph Stop that!

Pete *tries to stop crying.*

Pete I'll have to take the sticks off, no sense in wastin' 'em.

Pete *knocks the sticks out of the fire.*

Ralph I want your wife's baby Mr Bird, a straight swap. A baby for a job.

Pete *pauses for a moment, then brushes his fingers through his hair, touches the photograph and leaves.*

Scene Ten

Derbyshire. Golf course on high ground.

A golfer, **Judge Saxonbridge,** *is in a sand bunker. Her* **Caddy** *wears a yoke around his neck from which are hung golf clubs.*

Caddy Bastard int' it? E're try this.

He gives the **Judge** *a club.*

Judge You think? (*She takes up a stance.*)

Caddy Gotta let it know. I don't like the look of your knees mistress. That is you've got pretty knees, kneecaps like delicate china saucers, but your knees ain't positioned right.

Judge No?

Caddy No. So, did you hang 'im?

The **Judge** *readjusts her stance.*

Judge Is this better?

Caddy Feet more together.

Judge No, I didn't hang him. He was Section Fived.

Caddy Hard that, comin' from a two and going to a five.

Judge It was hard. I knew and liked Sandy, he was a good judge.

But buggery is against the law and Sandy was a bugger. Still *is* a bugger no doubt, I expect he's orientating himself in prison even as we speak. Finding out who's worth buggering and who's not.

Caddy Did you know 'e was an 'omo mistress?

Judge Of course. We turned a blind eye. Well until the silly bugger thrust his sexuality under our noses. Court Usher found him enjoying sexual congress with a young policeman. The wig and the helmet as one, hilarious sight apparently. When's my hair appointment?

Caddy Half past one with Mr Stephen. He done a good job last time.

The **Judge** *shrugs.*

Judge Do *your* job vassal, find me something to get this ball out of . . .

Ralph *and* **Pete** *enter.* **Ralph** *is in golfing clothes,* **Pete** *is laden, like the other caddy, with golf clubs on a yoke.*

Ralph (*delighted*) Judge Saxonbridge! Remember me? Ralph Darling?

The **Judge** *is not pleased.*

Ralph The club house, 1992. My wife won the raffle, and you presented the prize – a weekend in Penzance. We didn't go, a crisis at work. You sat down at our table and we had a drink and a brief conversation. No, don't remember? We talked about our respective cars.

Judge No, I don't remember . . .

Ralph You lost an ear-ring. It was later found in the car park, in the gutter. It was me who retrieved it.

Judge Yes. Remember now. You're in an extraordinary line of business aren't you?

Ralph No.

Judge Hand puppets, something otiose.

Ralph No, I manufacture drinking straws.

Judge Yes. How very picaresque of you. Now if you'd stand to one side . . .

Ralph My wife often talks about you . . .

Caddy (*to* **Ralph**) The judge is tryin' to concentrate. (*To* **Pete**.) What you doin' 'ere?

Pete I'm 'elpin' Mr Darling. 'E's playing a quick round until the bar opens and then we're going to see my wife, she's in hospital.

Caddy You ain't Class Four are you, servants and menials? You're a five ain't you?

Pete Yes.

Caddy Then you en't allowed to 'elp Mr Darling, and you also en't allowed anywhere near this golf course. (*To* **Judge**.) Mistress this man en't been vassalised.

Ralph He's got a one day pass.

Ralph *takes out the pass, shows it to the* **Judge**.

Judge (*impatiently*) But this is for Buxton, we are not *in* Buxton, merely on the outskirts. And, if this man is not your vassal then you had better remove him.

Ralph He's going to be!

Caddy That en't good enough! Is it mistress? Going to be, don't make it, 'is'.

Judge (*throwing her club down*) I came here to play golf (*She pronounces it 'goff'*), allow me to do so.

Caddy *picks up the club, gives it back to the* **Judge**.

Caddy Mistress, I beg to offer you advice, 'umble of course.

Judge Knees again?

Caddy No mistress, 'e shun't be 'ere – doin' a Four job, 'e shun't be doin' any job. If 'e's *'ere* what am I? An 'is paper, it's not right. As you said yerself, this ain't Buxton, we're three kilometres out. If some brown snout was to report it.

Pete I'm sorry if I've done sommat wrong, only I don't know the rules. If somebody will tell me what they are, I'll try and keep 'em.

Caddy They're not wrote down, the only way you find out what they are is when you break one, then you find out sharpish. But 'e should know 'em. (*Looking at* **Ralph**.) 'E's a Three. (*To* **Ralph**.) You should know 'em, and keep 'em.

Ralph (*to* **Judge**) Judge Saxonbridge should he be talking to me like this?

Judge He's my vassal. He knows how far to go.

Caddy You're only one up from me, Mr Darling.

Judge And one down from me, Mr Darling.

Caddy The *pig* in the middle.

The **Caddy** *and the* **Judge** *laugh.*

Caddy I'll take the Class Five away mistress.

Judge Good man.

Ralph (*throwing car keys*) Lock him in the car. I need him. (*To* **Pete.**) Remember the car you came in? So you can point it out to this vassal here?

Pete Was it a red one?

Pete *and the* **Caddy** *leave.*

Judge A red one! They live in the world of sights and sounds only. I sometimes envy them their simplicity.

Ralph He's fathered a baby, more than I can do.

Judge Illegally fathered?

Ralph I'm buying it off him. It's due this morning. A boy, an exceptional one. It was marked down for research but I got in first.

Judge (*to herself*) Knees. (*She misses the ball.*) Come on Saxonbridge! (*To* **Ralph.**) Mind caddying for me?

Ralph I'd like to Judge, but I'm a Three.

Judge It matters not a jot to me. I have no class consciousness. Wouldn't be a member here if I had.

Ralph I wondered about that. I think it's wonderful of you to mix with us Three's.

Judge Question of logistics.

Ralph Logistics?

Judge This course is equidistant. Home and Assizes. (*She points to her right and then to her left.*) Lovely spot though, used to be a nature reserve didn't it? Come on now Darling, do as I asked. (**Ralph** *picks up the yoke, puts it on his shoulders.*) Don't suppose you have the papers on you?

Ralph What papers?

Judge The papers assigning this baby over to you and your wife. I ask merely out of curiosity.

Ralph I've got a gentleman's agreement. And I'm paying good money. I don't need papers as well do I?

Judge You're undermining my whole existence Darling. Papers are the bedrock on which the legal profession is built.

Ralph It's a sort of private arrangement.

Judge It's a transaction, and any transaction be it a bundle of hay, an acre of land or a baby, requires an obligation that it be written down and witnessed should it be subsequently required by the judiciary.

Ralph I didn't think.

Judge Of course you didn't think. Ours is a totalitarian state, thinking is not exactly encouraged, indeed it is discouraged. Us Two's and Three's are lazy creatures anyway, not thinking suits us. That's why we are so awfully respectable. We take the easy line down the river, not for us the uncertainty of the rapids. Not like my vassal, if I said to him, 'Fancy going over Niagara Falls in a barrel?' He'd say, 'That sounds like a bit of fun mistress.' Y'see the lower classes *engage* in life. They have to, they haven't the vocabulary to avoid it.

Ralph You've got me worried now. You've set me *thinking*.

Judge (*laughing*) Don't start *thinking* Darling, not at this stage in the game.

The **Caddy** *arrives back.*

Caddy Mistress! What's this? Still in the sand?

Judge I blame my caddy, don't you vassal?

Caddy I do, 'e's a proper gorm face.

The **Judge** *and the* **Caddy** *laugh.*

Give me back my mistress's equipment.

Ralph *takes off the yoke and places it over the head of the* **Caddy**.

Judge Vassal, got a nice legal point. Are you up-to-date on your unborn child law?

Caddy I am. (*He taps his head.*)

Judge An unborn baby. A boy.

Caddy Yes.

Judge An illegal.

Caddy Shockin'.

Judge Once born, going to Government research, parents Class Fives.

Caddy I got you.

Judge Enter a third party.

Caddy Welcome aboard.

Judge Who wishes to purchase the unborn child.

Caddy Right.

Judge Much paperwork involved?

Caddy Oh yes. Paper, time and money. Child could be shavin' 'fore it's all done with, it is a boy en't it?

Ralph Well I wouldn't be going to all this trouble for a . . .

Caddy Girl, no. Begging your pardon mistress.

Ralph But what if I have a gentleman's agreement?

Judge Vassal?

Caddy You ain't a gentleman, neither is the true father, an' that child belongs to the Government, so it's them you got to deal with see? Here. (*He hands* **Ralph** *a paper.*) Subsection Five, Clause B1, of the Protection of the Unborn Child Act. Either that or you pay Judge Saxonbridge a lot of money. This won't do mistress, we got to get you out of the sand, 'ere try this. (*He passes the* **Judge** *a club.*) And how about putting your glasses on?

The **Judge** *fumbles for her glasses, puts them on.*

Judge Ah!

Caddy Now knees, feet an' give it a good thwonk.

The **Judge** *hits the ball and everyone watches its trajectory.*

Caddy Straight in the badgers set! Still the grey haired bastards are long gone. Ready for the next hole then judge?

Judge Yes, I'm rather pleased with that shot.

The **Judge** *and the* **Caddy** *start to move off.*

Ralph I'll pay Judge Saxonbridge.

Caddy It's easier. I wouldn't advise no one to tangle with the law. I'll send you an invoice.

Ralph Goodbye then Judge.

Judge Goodbye Darling, vassal sort you out all right?

Judge and **Caddy** *leave.*

Ralph Yes, I think.

Scene Eleven

Buxton Maternity Unit

Dot *and* **Lucinda***'s room now changed into a labour room. The beds are higher, firmer. Near to each other, against the same wall.*

Dot *and* **Lucinda** *are in* **Lucinda***'s bed together. They have their arms around each other. They are sitting up, looking ahead.*

Dot I shall have to move Luce, sorry.

Dot *takes her arms from around* **Lucinda** *and straightens up.*

Lucinda Did you feel her kicking?

Dot I did an' all. Did you feel him?

Lucinda (*imitating* **Dot**) I did an' all. (*They laugh.*) I don't know how we can laugh.

Dot No, but what else is there? We've done everything else. I'm worn out with it all.

Lucinda Do you remember how it was Dorothy, before the Sections?

Dot Yes, but it does no good remembering.

Lucinda Where did you live, before?

Dot In a street, in a town.

Lucinda In a house?

Dot A maisonette, ground floor, I lived with me mam and dad, and me brothers. It was all right, we had a bit of a garden.

Lucinda (*pleased*) A garden!

Dot Only a bit of one. After me dad died nobody did nothin' to it. It grew just the same. When it was hot we used to sit out in it, on a blanket on the grass, smokin' fags and talking.

Lucinda I miss cigarettes, do you?

Dot I miss readin' more.

Lucinda (*astonished*) Do you?

Dot I used to be a big reader, they used to say me 'ead would burst.

Lucinda Who did?

Dot Everybody.

Lucinda If I'd known you liked reading I'd have brought some books in.

Dot Have you got many?

Lucinda Oh I don't keep them in the house! I'd have bought them, from a shop.

Dot Thanks. Do they still have new ones, you know, coming out every year?

Lucinda I couldn't tell you Dorothy. I went through a phase of reading books. I'd be eighteen, but they made me think about too many things and my skin went to pieces, so my parents got rid of them. It was such a relief. Pass my make-up bag.

Dot *passes it to* **Lucinda**.

Dot (*bursting out*) What do you think they'll do with my baby Luce?

Lucinda You promised! You said you wouldn't talk about that! It was agreed between us. We talk about ante-natal not post-natal.

Dot I've got to talk, I can't keep it in. It's choking me.

Lucinda Don't Dorothy, I'm relying on you.

Dot They won't have him. They won't! The Government are not 'avin' my kid. And they're not 'avin' yours.

Lucinda Crudwell didn't say he was going to put Peter to sleep, and I'm sure, when it comes to the point, they won't be able to . . . kill Rosie. He was just showing off, like men do. He's an eccentric. Lots of clever professional men are.

The door opens, the **Orderly** *enters dressed in operating theatre clothes, pushing a small trolley.*

Orderly That's better! You look more like human beings now. I said to my colleague, 'If I'd wanted to work with wild animals I would have become a zoo keeper.' I've never seen anything to match it. The ugliness! The noise you were making. The lack of control, gulping, sobbing, moaning, ugh! The snot, the tears, your faces were completely distorted. You both came very near to being physically restrained.

Dot You're a very bad person.

Lucinda I'm very frightened of you.

Orderly Unless you were frightened of me I couldn't do my job could I? I need to feel contempt for you, and frightened people are totally contemptible, don't you think so? There's something about a bowed head that makes me want to kick it! Fortunately my job entails coping with weakness and pain and dependancy, so I'm fuelled throughout the day. As I said, it allows me to do my job.

Pause.

You had your baths?

Lucinda Yes.

Orderly Move your bed Mrs Bird. It's induction time.

Dot *climbs into her own bed.*

The **Orderly** *prepares two injections from the trolley. She talks as she works.*

Orderly I expect it's quite a novelty to have a daily bath isn't it Mrs Bird? You don't have piped water do you?

Dot We've got the river. We collect the rain.

Orderly Me and my friend drove to a Section Five Unit, a few years ago, for a laugh. It was a terrible place. As we were leaving a man threw himself under our car. A youngish man.

Lucinda I've never seen a Section Five Unit. But I absolutely know I could never live there.

The **Orderly** *picks up a syringe and goes to* **Lucinda**'s *bedside.* **Lucinda** *screams.*

Orderly It's only a hormone to start you off. (*She prepares* **Lucinda** *for injection, swabbing her arm.*) Still the Class Fives are slowly dying out. Another forty years and they'll be gone. I hope I live to see it. Pity I'll be old. It's going to be wonderful. Everybody beautiful and healthy, and intelligent and sensible, and working and earning money. Utopia. Pity I'll be old. (*She injects* **Lucinda**.)

Lucinda How long will it take?

Orderly You'll deliver at 11.59. Your husband will be here to hold your hand.

Lucinda I don't want him here. I want to hold Dot's hand.

Dot *extends her hand,* **Lucinda** *takes it.*

It's rough, like a pumice stone.

Dot I wish I had hands like yours.

The **Orderly** *prepares* **Dot** *for her injection.*

Lucinda I'm not going to be brave.

Orderly I can freeze your spinal cord. You won't feel a thing then.

Lucinda No, I want to feel something of her.

Dot *is injected.*

Orderly You'll deliver at twelve exactly.

Dot An' then what?

Orderly Don't ask me, I only fetch and carry. Your waters will break in half an hour. Why don't you stroll about until then?

Dot Where?

Orderly Back and forth, to and fro. Take your minds off the coming ordeal. (*An order.*) Put the coffee on.

Dot Coffee? How can we?

Orderly I was talking to a junior colleague. Your progress, and that of your babies is being monitored 24 hours a day. A recent medical innovation.

Dot Some folks might call it spyin'.

Lucinda Others, more articulate, may pronounce it to be an invasion of privacy.

Dot I don't like the idea of somebody watching me day and night. Your body's not your own is it?

Orderly We have no interest in your *body.* Only its functions, or more accurately its malfunctions.

Lucinda Is somebody watching us now?

The **Orderly** *smiles and waves to all corners of the room.*

Lucinda Is it a man or a woman?

Orderly Does it matter to you?

Lucinda Yes, actually it does.

Lucinda *takes a lipstick out of her make-up bag, applies it.*

The **Orderly** *stands and walks to the door. She turns.*

Orderly I don't know why. We've already got a list of every blemish, mark and varicose vein on your body. (*She goes out.*)

Dot *and* **Lucinda** *gaze around the room, trying to locate the video cameras. But they are undetectable.*

Dot They don't know what we're thinking Luce, they can't get inside our heads. (*Pause.*) Not yet.

Lucinda (*loud whisper*) Dot, friends are allowed to live together aren't they?

Dot So long as they're the same class.

Lucinda I could drop two classes Dot. I could come and live with you.

Dot And Pete?

Lucinda I'd forgotten about him.

Dot I haven't.

Lucinda All right, with Pete.

Dot You wouldn't last five minutes Luce. You don't know.

Lucinda Tell me, I'll prepare myself.

Dot It's like half-living.

Lucinda I'm used to that!

Dot And it's hard, hard as concrete. Hard on the body and hard on the mind.

Lucinda I'm an adaptable person.

Dot It's not what I want for you. Not now we're friends. I don't want the shine taken off you.

Lucinda Too late, it's already gone.

Dot It was strange coming through Buxton in the police car. The people had smooth faces and they were all good looking, life hadn't touched them and left its mark. And their clothes! Soft, in colours like those bottled sweets. And proper shoes in all sorts of shapes. I looked out at them through the car window and I felt like an animal. You didn't see the clothes I came in with did you?

Lucinda No.

Dot They took them away and burnt them. They wore rubber gloves. But the people in Buxton Lucinda! They were so beautiful. Walking and talking so straight and happy, shining hair and clean hands. And I saw some children, and dogs on leads, and shops with food spilling out onto the pavement. And people buying, choosing. And all the time talking in these soft voices as if they didn't know about people like me and Pete.

Lucinda They're Section Threes, the people you saw.

Dot Lucinda, I want to be one. I want to be like you. I want to go shopping in Buxton.

Lucinda Manchester's better, for shopping.

Dot Is it?

Lucinda You can't get fresh coriander in Buxton.

Dot And that's bad is it?

Lucinda Yes, if you're at all interested in adventurous cooking.

Dot I could be interested. I want to be interested. So I'd have to go to Manchester?

Lucinda Yes, in a car.

Dot Yes. To sink into a car seat and just let your legs flop. And you just stare out of the window and look at the weather (*Bitterly.*) instead of being *in it* all the time, getting wet and counting the steps uphill. You're there so quickly in a car. And then you've got time.

Lucinda Time to do what?

Dot Go shopping. With money in your hand. Hard coins and soft paper. Lucinda I want *things*. I want to go in shops and walk about like I'm in a dream – like the people in Buxton. How can I get money Lucinda?

Lucinda You can't. You'll never have any money. You're a Five.

Dot I want things!

Lucinda Stop it Dot.

Dot (*shouting*) Why can't I have them? I'm as good as you.

Lucinda You're making yourself unhappy now.

Dot I want something nice next to my skin.

Lucinda You'll forget all about Buxton once you're back in the countryside.

Dot No, I won't. I'll keep that memory going. I'll exercise it and keep it fresh.

Ralph *enters.*

Ralph (*to* **Dot**) You're holding my wife's hand.

Dot She's holding mine.

Ralph (*to* **Lucinda**) Let it go!

Ralph *rushes to separate the hands. He holds* **Lucinda**'s *hand.*

Lucinda You're hurting me!

Ralph You're to have no more contact with her, physical or otherwise. (*He looks at his watch.*) I'm not even allowing idle talk about domestic appliances.

Dot I wouldn't know where to begin.

Long pause.

Ralph Talk to me Lucinda. I'm a visitor at your bedside.

Lucinda I don't want to talk to you.

Ralph You're a Government woman. You have to talk to me. You have to ask me about my work, sympathise about the many and varied problems I encounter in the competitive world of straw manufacturing.

Lucinda I couldn't be less interested. I've always thought it was a silly way to make a living. It's not as if people *need* them is it? If all the drinking straws vanished overnight it wouldn't matter would it? The sun would still come up, the stars would appear in the night sky. The earth would not stop turning Ralph.

Pete *enters, he is dressed in hospital clothing. He has just had a bath. His hair is wet.*

Pete Where's Dot?

Dot Pete!

Pete You're there!

He rushes to **Dot***'s bedside. He stands looking down at her.*

Pete They made me have a bath, they said I smelled. I don't know where me clothes are. I shall need 'em to go home in.

Dot It's the smoke from the fire, we don't notice, bein' in it all the time.

Pete We don't look like us do we?

Dot But we still are us. (*She puts her arms out, and they embrace.*) You shouldn't be 'ere. How did you get in without a pass?

Pete Mr Darling fetched me. He got the paper and everything. I've bin' in 'is car.

Lucinda Ralph! That was kind. Uncharacteristically so,

Ralph I had a business proposition to put to Mr Bird.

Pete 'E's givin' me a job Dot! In Buxton.

Dot A job? Pete! Oh I'm so 'appy for you. What job is it?

Pete I don't know, but I can turn my hand to owt can't I? I told 'im that. 'E knows about the readin' an' writin'. No sense in coverin' up.

Dot (*to* **Ralph**) What job is it?

Ralph I'll find him something to do . . .

Pete See, I told you. It's true.

Dot How will he get to work? There's no buses where we live.

Ralph He's prepared to walk.

Dot Across the moors? There and back?

Pete I can do it. I'm a good walker. It's only four mile there and four mile back.

Dot (*to* **Ralph**) He'll need boots for that.

Pete I'll save up and buy some from a shop. I'm goin' to buy you a present when I get my wages. Something nice, something surprisin'.

Dot (*to* **Ralph**) If you let him down . . .

Ralph We've signed a contract.

Pete 'E told me what it said.

Dot Where *is* this contract? Can I see it?

Ralph No, Mr Crudwell is perusing it.

Lucinda What business is it of Crudwell's who you employ?

Pause.

Ralph (*to* **Pete**) You tell her, she's your wife.

Pete (*to* **Dot**) Mr Darling come this morning. I were just lightin' the fire. We talked a bit. Then, he said he'd give me *a job*. Only thing is 'e wants the baby.

Dot What baby?

Pete (*Pointing to* **Dot***'s belly.*) That one.

There is a long pause, **Dot** *and* **Pete** *stare at each other.*

Lucinda What do you propose to do with Dot's baby Ralph?

Ralph Keep it and bring it up as my son. Teach it to speak grammatically and respect the Government. He'll stand when you, his mother, comes into the room. I have my ambitions for him. I'm hoping he'll achieve Class Two status before he's 35.

Dot (*to* **Pete**) You've gev' 'im away?

Pete I 'ad to, for the job.

Lucinda I don't want him.

Ralph You'll learn to want him Lucinda. Crudwell tells me he's exceptionally intelligent. They had him earmarked for experimental use, but I've negotiated a price and he's ours. It'll mean cutting down a bit. He wasn't cheap.

Ralph *goes to* **Dot***'s bed and stands over her.*

Ralph So he's mine. (*He puts his hands on her belly.*) Won't be long son, you'll soon be in your daddy's arms.

Scene Twelve

The delivery room

Sound of a foetal heartbeat.

Crudwell, **Pete** *and* **Ralph** *have their backs to the audience. Only the men are on stage. They are cheering and shouting as though they are at a sporting function. A foetal heartbeat is heard throughout. Very loud. They are watching* **Dot***'s baby being born.* **Ralph** *carries a bottle of champagne by its neck. The*

*speed of the heartbeat increases, then suddenly stops. The baby is born. The
men cheer. They swig champagne. They leave, excited and happy.*

Scene Thirteen

A few minutes later

Lucinda *and* **Dot** *are tired, they have given birth, they are holding hands.
The* **Orderly** *comes in and starts to tidy the room.*

Lucinda My baby, is she pretty?

Orderly Not especially.

Lucinda I want to see her. Make sure she's all right.

Orderly She's not all right. She's dead. She had nine toes. So she's
dead. (*Pause.*) I was only doing my job.

Lucinda (*covering her face*) I want to see her.

Orderly There's no point, she's dead. (*Angry.*) She's well out of it!
Since when has living been so marvellous? I can't remember the last
time I woke up and welcomed the day.

Dot Where's my baby? Where's Peter?

Orderly Peter is being christened, in champagne. He's a lovely
baby. (*To* **Lucinda**.) Cheer up Mrs Darling, you won't be going
home with empty arms will you? You'll have Peter.

Ralph *and* **Pete** *burst in.* **Ralph** *holds the baby,* **Peter**, *above his head.*

Ralph My son! My son! He's got ten fingers, ten toes and balls like
a prize bull.

Dot (*alarmed*) Put him down! You'll drop him! Give him to me!

Pete I've held him Dot. He's 'eavy, eight pound fifteen ounces.

Dot (*screams*) Give him to me, he's mine.

Lucinda Give him to Dot!

Ralph (*to* **Lucinda**) He's yours and he's mine. I've paid and I've
got the papers. (*He puts the baby into* **Lucinda**'s *arms.*)

Lucinda Look Dot. He's beautiful. Look at his fingernails.

Dot (*craning to look*) Let me hold him Lucinda.

Ralph No! He stays with his mother.

Dot Let me Mr Darling. (**Dot** *touches the baby's face.*)

Pete He's lovely an' he's got my name.

Ralph Correction, he's got my name, Ralph. Ralph Darling the second. Darling and Son, Drinking Straws. The delivery vans will be repainted, overnight.

Pete Is that what I'll be doing, driving a van for you? Is that what my job'll be, driving a van?

Ralph Tell you what Pete, you start walking back to Axley Edge eh? I'll contact you when I've got a vacancy eh?

Pete Few days?

Ralph Longer than a few days.

Pete A week then?

Ralph Could be a bit longer than a week. We'll be busy, with the baby.

Pete (*getting anxious*) A month then?

Dot Never. He'll never give you a job. You gave our baby away for nought. And now you've got nought left, because you've lost me an' all.

Pete Don't shout Dot, you'll wake the baby!

Lucinda (*to* **Ralph**) I shall need to employ a wet nurse Ralph. I don't intend to lose my figure, or my sleep. Dot can feed the baby, she's already lost her figure so it doesn't matter. Take her husband home. Let *him* drive, with a bit of luck you'll go off the road and both be killed.

Ralph You've just given birth, so I'll forget you spoke to me like that.

Pete (*to* **Dot**) So when you coming home then?

Dot (*deliberately*) I'll come home the day he gives you a job.

Pete Right, well I'll see you . . . it shouldn't be too long.

He kisses **Dot**. *She does not respond.*
Ralph *kisses* **Lucinda**, *she does not respond.*

Ralph *and* **Pete** *leave.*

Lucinda *passes the baby to* **Dot**.

Dot *puts him to the breast. She puts her cheek down to touch his.*

Dot I want him all to myself.

Lucinda So do I. I'll be jealous. It's going to be very difficult.

The **Orderly** *enters carrying a baby in a blanket.*

Orderly (*to* **Lucinda**) Your daughter. She's still warm.

Lucinda Thank you.

Orderly (*Pause.*) I shouldn't be doing this.

She puts the baby into **Lucinda**'s *arms.*

Dot She *is* pretty.

Orderly Thirty seconds. I shouldn't be doing this.

Lucinda *unwraps the coverings around the baby, examines the baby carefully.*

Dot She's not just pretty Lucinda, she's beautiful. And do you know what I like best about her?

Lucinda Her feet?

Dot Yes, her feet.

Orderly There's been all hell let loose about this toe. The sperm bank blaming Crudwell, him blaming them. It's supposed to be infallible.

Dot What's your name?

Orderly Orderly, that's my name. Fetch this, carry that. I work with the snot, the shit and the vomit. I haven't got a name, not here.

Lucinda Everybody's got a name.

Orderly My mother didn't have one. Her name was Susan, but nobody called her that. She was Mrs Meadowcroft to the neighbours, and she was 'mother' to me.

Dot What is your name?

Orderly Anne Louise. (*Pause.*) She died last month.

Dot I'm sorry.

Orderly I'm sorry. (*Pause.*) I'll have to take her. There are procedures, timings. If I don't keep to them, I'll be lost.

Lucinda *Her* name is Rosie.

Orderly Rosie Darling, right. I know a nice place for her. (*She leaves.*)

Lucinda Dot, I don't care about my figure. My breasts have already drooped, it's only wire and padding that's been keeping them perky.

Dot We can make a good bloke out of this baby Luce. Teach him things. Get some books in the house. Look at him, he's a lump of clay.

Lucinda I used to be good at pottery, I went to classes. I made some beautiful things.

Dot *He'll* be beautiful an' all. Nice to know, kind but not scared. He'll walk for miles, he'll know how to look after himself.

Lucinda He won't care how many toes a person has got. Dot I'm leaking, my milk has come through.

Dot *removes the baby.*

Dot Mummy's turn.

Dot *hands the baby to* **Lucinda** *who puts the baby to her breast.*

Printed in the United Kingdom
by Lightning Source UK Ltd.
122857UK00001B/436-441/A